Contents

The building site

There used to be a wasteground across from my house.
But then the builders came . . .

Watch Out!
Builders About!

Mick Manning
and Brita Granström

W
FRANKLIN WATTS
LONDON•SYDNEY

For Melker Granström with love

First published in 2002
by Franklin Watts,
96 Leonard Street,
London EC2A 4XD

Franklin Watts Australia
56 O'Riordan Street
Alexandria
NSW 2015

The illustrations in this book
have been drawn by Brita

Text and illustrations © 2002 Mick Manning
and Brita Granström
Series editor: Rachel Cooke
Art director: Jonathan Hair

Printed in Hong Kong, China
A CIP catalogue record is available from
the British Library.
Dewey Classification 690
ISBN 0 7496 4298 X

Lots of different people work on a building site. First architects and surveyors plot and plan, then the brickies and labourers get started.

BUILDER

A digger flattened the ground.
Some people measured
and set out pegs.

Surveyors 'set out' the architect's
plans with pegs and string.
The builders use these as a guide
when they start digging.

Foundations

The next day, the digger dug and scooped. 'They're the foundations,' the foreman said.

Buildings have foundations dug deep into the ground to make sure they stand upright and don't fall down.

Building sites are dangerous. Never go to one on your own or without permission.

Then came the
cement mixer.
Runny concrete
glooped and gooed
from a pipe -
slipping and sliding
into the holes . . .

The foundations are filled as soon as possible with ready-mixed concrete. Once it has dried, the bricks are laid on top.

13

Deliveries!

Huge trucks came, with
bricks, concrete, planks,
beams and window frames.
How would they use all of it?

It's not just bricks that get delivered: tiles, pipes, even walls, floors, windows and doors come to the site ready-made.

Uniloaders shifted breeze
blocks, bricks and roof tiles.
The walls grew higher.

With a clank and a clang,
the scaffolding went up.

Scaffolding clips and bolts together to make a safe platform for the builders to work on as the building grows.

Build it higher!

A crowd gathered to watch a giant crane - hooking and lifting, dangling and lowering.

In modern buildings, floors are made from slabs of concrete which slot in as the walls go up. You need a crane to put them in position.

19

The street was filled with noise! Whining saws, banging hammers, whistling workers!

There is lots of team work on a building site. The foreman is like the captain, who makes sure everyone is in the right place at the right time and knows what to do.

Look inside

One day, Mum and Dad took me to look around inside . . . There were lots of stairs and great big windows. I liked it!

Safety is very important on building sites. Safety helmets have to be worn at all times in case of falling bricks – imagine if someone dropped a hammer!

23

All sorts of things are hidden inside a building's floors and walls: pipes for water and heating, wires for electric lights and sockets.

Electricians were
putting in the
wiring. Plumbers
were fitting the
pipes. Decorators
were painting.
Dad winked at me.

Dad's surprise

Now the view from my window has changed. We've moved into our brand new home.

And my old house? Well, the builders have moved in!

Building ideas

Find out more about building by designing a new, one-storey home of your own.

Make a home

Take a shoe box and paint the outside with either brick, stone or wood effects. Don't forget to paint in windows and doors!

Make the roof like this using the lid and an extra piece of card. Paint it with grey slates or red pantiles. The roof is easy to lift on and off.

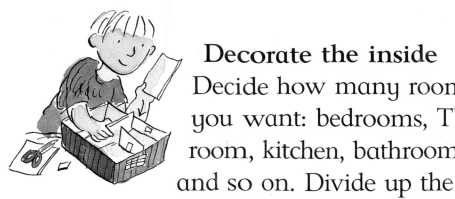

Decorate the inside

Decide how many rooms you want: bedrooms, TV room, kitchen, bathroom, and so on. Divide up the rooms with cardboard walls.

You can decorate the inside of your 'house' using paints or even wallpaper. Now move in! You can use some play figures.

Safety

It is fun to watch builders at work but always do so from a safe distance. Never try to visit a building site on your own without an adult. Maybe ask the foreman to show you around.

29

Building words and index

architect A person who designs a building and draws up plans for builders to follow. Pages 7, 9

brickies Builders who specialise in laying bricks. Page 7

concrete A strong, long-lasting material made from a mixture of sand, gravel and cement. Pages 12, 13, 14, 19

electrician A person who fits the electrical parts in a building and mends them if they go wrong. Page 25

foreman The person on a building site who organises the other builders and tells them what to do. Pages 10, 21

foundations The base of a building, usually under the ground, which makes sure it stands up straight and will not fall down easily. Pages 10, 11, 13

labourer A person who does all the general lifting and moving work on a building site. Page 7

plumber A person who fits all the pipes that move water around a building and mends them if they go wrong. Page 25

scaffolding A frame of pipes and planks put around a building so you can work high up safely. Pages 16, 17

surveyor A person who makes sure that land is good to build on and that the architect's plans are safely and correctly carried out. Pages 7, 9

uniloader A big machine used to move and shift piles of bricks and other heavy loads. Page 16